Samuel Beckett's

Waiting for Godot

Text by
Rita Wilensky
(M.S., Ed., Lehman College)
Instructor of Reading
Intermediate School 193
Bronx, New York

Illustrations by
Curtis Perone

 Research & Education Association

Library of Congress Catalog Card Number 96-67420

International Standard Book Number 0-87891-057-3

MAXnotes® is a registered trademark of
Research & Education Association, Piscataway, New Jersey 08854

I-1

What **MAXnotes®** Will Do for You

This book is intended to help you absorb the essential contents and features of Samuel Beckett's *Waiting for Godot* and to help you gain a thorough understanding of the work. The book has been designed to do this more quickly and effectively than any other study guide.

For best results, this **MAXnotes** book should be used as a companion to the actual work, not instead of it. The interaction between the two will greatly benefit you.

To help you in your studies, this book presents the most up-to-date interpretations of every section of the actual work, followed by questions and fully explained answers that will enable you to analyze the material critically. The questions also will help you to test your understanding of the work and will prepare you for discussions and exams.

Meaningful illustrations are included to further enhance your understanding and enjoyment of the literary work. The illustrations are designed to place you into the mood and spirit of the work's settings.

The **MAXnotes** also include summaries, character lists, explanations of plot, and section-by-section analyses. A biography of the author and discussion of the work's historical context will help you put this literary piece into the proper perspective of what is taking place.

The use of this study guide will save you the hours of preparation time that would ordinarily be required to arrive at a complete grasp of this work of literature. You will be well prepared for classroom discussions, homework, and exams. The guidelines that are included for writing papers and reports on various topics will prepare you for any added work which may be assigned.

The **MAXnotes** will take your grades "to the max."

Dr. Max Fogiel
Program Director

Contents

**Each Act includes List of Characters,
Summary, Analysis, Study Questions and
Answers, and Suggested Essay Topics.**

Introduction

The Life and Work of Samuel Beckett

"I have a clear memory of my own fetal existence. It was an existence where no voice, no possible movement could free me from the agony and darkness I was subjected to." So says Samuel Barclay Beckett who was born on or about Good Friday, April 13, 1906. He was born in Foxrock, a suburb of Dublin, Ireland, in a large house called Cooldrinagh.

Here, in this secluded three story Tudor home, surrounded by acres of gardens, a croquet lawn, stables for his mother's donkeys and dogs, a hen house, and a tennis court, Beckett and his older brother spent their childhood. High brick walls separated them from the outside world, and ensured them uninterrupted tea parties, piano lessons, and formal dinners.

Their much-loved father took them hiking and swimming. Their mother, against whom Beckett rebelled almost all of his life, took them to church. By the time they were five, the boys were in school. By the time they were 12, they were local tennis champions—aiming all shots at their opponents' heads.

Before he left for boarding school in 1920, Beckett had already developed into an avid reader. He kept his books on a small shelf above his bed, along with busts of Shakespeare and Dante. At boarding school, he excelled at sports, and received a solid educational foundation. He entered Trinity College (Dublin) in 1923.

There he became an intellectual. He read Descartes, French poetry, Rimbaud, Baudelaire, and Apollinaire, and discovered the theatre of O'Casey and Pirandello. He was also rebellious and moody. He had a reputation for reckless driving, heavy drinking, and irreverent behavior. In spite of this, he graduated first in his class in 1927 with a major in modern languages.

In preparation for a teaching career at Trinity, Beckett went to France, where he worked with James Joyce, did research on René Descartes, and won a prize for his poem, *Whoroscope*. He wrote a study on Proust, noting: "We are alone. We cannot know, and we cannot be known;" and "There is no communication because there are no vehicles of communication."

Living by these words, he resigned from teaching once he received his M.A. degree from Trinity in 1931. He had hated it, and his students characterized him thus: "An exhausted aesthete who all life's poisonous wines had sipped, and found them rather tedious."

By the time his father died in 1933, leaving him a small income, Beckett's character had already been formed. Between bouts with physical and mental illnesses that included flus, colds, aching joints, depression, anxiety, boils, cysts, constipation, insomnia, and glaucoma in both eyes, he would live the rest of his life as a writer.

In the next fifty years he would go on to produce an impressive collection of work in a variety of genres. He created essays, poems, short stories, novels, plays, mime, and film. In 1969, he was awarded the Nobel Prize for Literature.

In December 1989, after too long a stay in "an old crock's home," Samuel Beckett died of respiratory failure at the age of 83. Right before he died, he was asked if anything in life was worthwhile. "Precious little," he replied.

Before attempting to make any sense out of *Waiting for Godot*, it is necessary to put some things into perspective. When Beckett wrote this play (from October 1948 to January 1949), he was already more than forty years old. Half of his life had passed. He considered himself a novelist who wrote *Godot #1* "as a form of relaxation, to get away from the awful prose I was writing at the time." It was like a game to him, a momentary release from the real work of constructing fiction. It was not the vehicle he would have chosen to make him famous.

However, once it was performed in 1953, it did make him famous. It inspired an abundance of critical comment, explanation and exegesis in a relatively short time. It became a contemporary classic.

Beckett consistently refused to comment on, or explain his work to the public. "My work is a matter of fundamental sounds (no joke intended) made as fully as possible, and I accept responsibility for nothing else. If people want to have headaches among the overtones, let them. And provide their own aspirin."

Beckett maintained control over his text throughout his life. Originally writing it in French, he translated it for an English-speaking audience, and both translated and directed the German production in 1975. He had it memorized and, when appropriate, changed some of the dialogue and stage direction himself. He wanted to "get it right", he said. He was not alone in this. Over the years, the material has been scrutinized by experts with their own biases, all trying to get it right.

There is a story in Beckett's novel, *Watt*, written in 1942, about a Mr. Ash, who goes to a great deal of trouble to check his watch (one similar to the one that reappears in Pozzo's pocket) for the exact time. "Seventeen minutes past five exactly, as God is my witness," he says. However, right at that moment Big Ben, the official clock of Westminster, strikes six. "This in my opinion is the type of all information whatsoever, be it voluntary or solicited," Beckett's narrator concludes. If you want a stone, ask a turnover. If you want a turnover, ask plum pudding."

This story characterizes some of the critics, as well as some of the interpretations of *Waiting for Godot*. It has been seen as existentialist (depicting man as lost as insecure in a world without God); Marxist (representing man turning away from his capitalist society, and embracing socialism and communism as alternatives to political alienation); Freudian (Vladimir represents the 'ego', Estragon represents the 'id'); and Christian (the play as a parable illustrating man's need for salvation). Yet, while these theories have some validity, they are all open to debate. They reflect a complex culture but limit understanding of the play. "The great success of *Waiting for Godot*," Beckett said, "had arisen from a misunderstanding: critic and public alike were busy interpreting in allegorical or symbolic terms a play which strove at all costs to avoid definition."

The inspiration for *Godot* may be found in the work of the late nineteenth-century symbolist playwrights. A description of symbolist drama, written by Remy de Gourmont in 1895, (which was also referred to as "static drama"), seems to have some relevance:

> Hidden in mist somewhere there is an island, and on that island there is a castle, and in that castle there is a great room lit by a little lamp. And in that room people are waiting. Waiting for what? They don't know! They're waiting for someone to open the door, waiting for their lamp to go out, waiting for Fear and Death. They talk. Yes, they speak words that shatter the silence of the moment. And then they listen again, leaving their sentences unfinished, their gesture uncomplicated. They are listening. They are waiting. Will she come perhaps, or won't she? Yes, she will come; she always comes. But it is late, and she will not come perhaps until tomorrow. The people collected under that little lamp in that great room have, nevertheless, begun to smile; they still have hope. Then there is a knock - a 'knock' and that is all there is: And it is Life Complete, All of Life.

While it may be helpful to examine the roots of Beckett's work, it is also necessary to mention that a new category was invented by critics of the fifties and sixties to house *Waiting for Godot*. This category, Theater of the Absurd, was used to describe the new kind of theater that Beckett represented. While Martin Esslin defined it as "striving to express its sense of the senselessness of the human condition and the inadequacy of the rational approach by the open abandonment of rational devices and discursive thought," other critics had their own interpretations. They characterized it as having absurd dialogue, characters and situations. It included the work of dramatists as diverse as Jean Genet, Harold Pinter, Edward Albee and Eugene Ionesco.

Some critics referred to Eugene Ionesco as the Grand Master of the Theater of the Absurd. His play, *The Bald Soprano,* produced in Paris three years before *Waiting for Godot,* ran for twenty years and was the first example of the "anti-theater theater." Although it seemed to follow the outline for light comedy by using a drawing room setting, it quickly transformed the clichéd dialogue of two model British families into madness and hysteria. This was absurdity in its typical sense, as hilarious farce.

This was not the kind of absurdity represented by Beckett, whose work was characterized by despair and deprivation. His work more closely resembles Camus' idea of the Absurd in *The Myth of Sisyphus*. Beckett's characters live in a world that no longer makes sense, that has no God, and offers no easy answers or solutions. Godot never comes. Kierkegaard (1813-1835), in a more Christian sense, labeled this Despair.

Ionesco once remarked, "I started writing for the theater because I hated it." Beckett's thoughts went even deeper. In his novel, *Molloy*, his character states, "You would do better, at least no worse, to obliterate texts than to blacken margins, to fill in the holes of words till all is blank and flat and the whole ghastly business looks like what it is, senseless, speechless, issueless misery."

Ionesco made every attempt to explain himself and his work to the public. Beckett did just the opposite. He resisted the impulse to explain or categorize his material. In fact, he abhorred all attempts to do so. He wanted form and content to remain inseparable, and the reading or experience of his work to speak for itself.

Although he attempted to be silent on the subject of his own work, agreeing with the French poet Baudelaire (1821-1867), about "the devastating vanity and uselessness of explaining anything to anyone," Beckett wrote literary criticism. Initially, he did it for the money, and toyed with the idea of making it a career. His essay on Joyce for *Our Exagmination*, his book on Proust, and his reviews for the *Bookman* and the *Criterion*, were all commissioned.

After 1934, however, Beckett's criticism became more personal. He wrote in defense of friends and fellow artists who were unjustly attacked or ignored. At one point, railing against the idea that art has a primary duty to be clear and accessible, Beckett wrote: "The time is not perhaps altogether too green for the vile suggestion that art has nothing to do with clarity, does not dabble in the clear and does not make clear."

In his essay on Joyce, Beckett wrote "no language is so sophisticated as English—it is abstracted to death," and claimed that the public's inability to understand information stems from being "too decadent to receive it." In another instance, he attacked the average reader by writing, "This rapid skimming and absorption of the scant cream of sense is made possible by what I may call a continuous process of copious intellectual salivation."

The essay on Proust was Beckett's critical masterpiece. In it he establishes his own basic philosophy about the inability to understand experience because of the dearth of methods for expression. He blames this on Time ("that double-headed monster of damnation and salvation"), Memory ("yesterday has deformed us or been deformed by us"), and Habit ("the ballast that chains a dog to his vomit").

Throughout his life, Samuel Beckett also wrote poetry. In 1930, he received first prize in a contest conducted by the Hours Press for his 98 line poem *Whoroscope*. This poem was based on the life of René Descartes (1596-1650), a French philosopher and mathematician. Although it was praised for its swift and witty language, the poem was difficult to interpret. Beckett was asked to provide explanatory footnotes for it, which he did. Clearly, at that point in his life, he was compliant.

He continued to write poetry through the 1930s and 1940s in both English and French. Then, in 1974, after a break of twenty-five years, he began to publish poetry again.

Before, during, and after *Waiting for Godot*, Beckett wrote novels. His first published novel *Murphy* (1938), was one of grotesque but comic action, and included characters such as Miss Rosie Dew, Miss Carridge, Augustus Tinklepenny, Bim and Bom, Dr. Killiecrankie, and Murphy, who takes a job at the Magdalen Mental Mercyseat. At the end of the novel, Murphy dies accidentally. Although his last request is to be cremated and have his ashes flushed down the toilet of the Abbey Theater, they remain scattered on the floor of a saloon.

From 1942 to 1944, while living in Roussillon, Beckett wrote *Watt*, which included veiled autobiographical accounts of his life. The main character is a patient in an asylum, who dictates his story to a fellow patient in a confusing language with a distorted chronology. A note in the addendum of *Watt* gives a sense of Beckett's paradoxical humour. "The following precious and illuminating material should be carefully studied. Only fatigue and disgust prevented its incorporation."

Watt was not designed for a postwar public's reading pleasure. It did not get published until 1953, and it was immediately banned in Ireland. This did not prevent Beckett, the novelist, from continuing on. His next novel was *Molloy* (1947), the first of a trilogy that was to include *Malone meurt* and *L'Innommable*.

Molloy is presented in two phases with two stories—one about Molloy, and the other about Moran. Both characters suffer from paralysis. When Molloy speaks, it is difficult to know whether events are real or imagined. Boundaries between his conscious and unconscious mind are blurred. When Moran speaks, everything he says is immediately cancelled, and nothing that happens is to be believed. This novel was referred to by critics as an "epic of the absurd," taking place in a "void" and outlining disintegration—of the heroes, of time, and of life.

Malone meurt was the book Beckett was writing in 1948 when he took his break and created *Godot*. Apparently Beckett's friends and family were worried that the introductory sentences in this novel, "I shall soon be quite dead at last in spite of all. Perhaps next month," applied to Beckett himself. They insisted that he stop writing and rest. Whether or not he was heeding their advice, he did humor himself by writing *Godot*, "to get away from the awful prose I was writing at the time."

Critics assumed that the philosophical underpinnings of *Malone meurt* were from the writings of Descartes (1596-1650), who wrote about the supposed split between the physical/mechanical and the mental/spiritual universes. There was also the influence of Geulinex (1624-1669), who wrote "Where you are worth nothing, there you should want nothing;" and Berkeley (1685-1753), who said there is no reality except in the mind.

Beckett, as usual, responded by claiming, "I don't know where the writing comes from and I am often quite surprised when I see what I have committed to paper."

His novels end with failure or death, the concept of "lessness is part of them". They become more and more difficult to follow as the humor is engulfed by tragedy, and the language is used to imitate what is being narrated. When Malone dies, his pencil finally gives out along with his consciousness:

> or with it or with his hammer or with his stick or with his
> fist or in thought in dream I mean never he will never
> or with his pencil or with his stick or

or light light I mean
never there he will never
never anything
there
any more

The last book of the trilogy, *L'Innommable*, completed in 1950, begins with a character who is neither male nor female, has no nose, and cannot move. All it does is sit in a jar with its hands on its knees, narrating a story which ends with the paradox, "I can't go on, I'll go on."

After the success of *Waiting for Godot*, Beckett wrote more plays. "The best possible play is one in which there are no actors, only the text. I'm trying to think of a way to write one," he said.

True to his word, he attempted to eliminate his characters. While *Waiting for Godot* had five actors, *Endgame* (1958) had only four. One character was dying, and two others were consigned to ashcans. The stage poem, "Play" (1964), was down to three performers, all stashed away in funereal urns. *Happy Days* (1961) had a woman buried to her waist and then her head in sand. Her husband remained invisible until he crawled out of his hole to say hello.

Krapp's Last Tape (1960) was a monologue with a single actor. *Breath*, first performed in 1969, had entirely buried its protagonist in a pile of garbage or expelled him to the wings. Even that was too much for Beckett, who then reverted to body parts. In *Not I* (1972), there is nothing but a blackened stage and a lit-up pair of lips.

Historical Background

Samuel Beckett lived from 1906 until 1989, during which time the world went through enormous social, cultural, and political changes.

Socially, Beckett was born into a privileged Anglo-Irish Protestant family whose household seemed unaffected by the changes around it. However, as a child, he witnessed first-hand the destruction and devastation caused by the Easter Rebellion of 1916 in Dublin.

As a young adult, he was exposed to the leading literary and political figures in Dublin. The pubs overlapped the world created by language and theater. He frequented the Abbey Theatre, home of Irish Nationalism, the Gate, home of experimental European drama, and the Queens Theatre, which was the center for melodrama. Beckett also got a taste of vaudeville; he loved the movies of Laurel and Hardy, Charlie Chaplin, and, later, the Marx Brothers.

When censorship renewed itself in Ireland in the late 1920s, and Beckett's book, *More Pricks Than Kicks*, came under attack, the stage was set for his subsequent move to France. He delighted in saying how he preferred "France in war to Ireland in peace," even though he had been stabbed on a Paris street for no apparent reason in 1938.

Fiercely protective of his private life, especially his relationship and marriage to Suzanne Deschevaux-Dumesnil, and not wanting to utter "another blot on silence," Beckett claimed to be apolitical. However, his actions proved otherwise. He openly attacked antisemitism, worked with the French Resistance during World War II, and joined an Irish Red Cross unit after the war to set up a hospital in Normandy.

In 1946, he began his most productive period. He wrote in French, perhaps in an attempt to "strip his language to the bare essentials of his vision." The world had come to a temporary resting point, only to succumb again to the endless recurrent political battles of a "post-nuclear age." In a world where traditional values and beliefs were under intense scrutiny, life seldom resembled a tidy, well-constructed play. In fact, it may have provided the right climate for *Waiting for Godot.*

En attendant Godot, (Waiting for Godot), was first presented on January 5, 1953, at the Babylone Theatre in Paris, France, to a packed house of more than 200 people. It had been financed by a small, state grant obtained by its producer, Roger Blin. Although the general public and conventional press winced in confusion over its meaning, it received enough praise from the "right" people to ensure its success.

In her review for *La Liberation,* Sylvain Zegel wrote: "Paris had just recognized in Samuel Beckett one of today's best playwrights". At 47, Beckett had become famous, and the phrase, "waiting for Godot," became an everyday expression of political cartoonists throughout the world.

The English version of *Waiting for Godot* opened in London at the Arts Theatre Club on August 3, 1955. Although the popular press initially dismissed it as "rubbish," leading theater critics jumped to its rescue. As a result, it managed to play to capacity audiences until May, 1956. When it opened in Dublin, it received more favorable reviews.

Waiting for Godot had its premiere in the United States at the Coconut Grove Playhouse in Miami, Florida on January 3, 1956. Reviewers hated it, and audiences walked out. The running joke was that the only place to be sure of finding a cab in Miami was outside of the theater, between acts.

The play got a better reception when it opened on Broadway, in April 1956. It was publicized as entertainment for "thoughtful and discriminating" audiences. In his review for *The New York Times*, Brooks Atkinson wrote, "Theater goers can rail at it, but they cannot ignore it. For Mr. Beckett is a valid writer."

Since then, *Waiting for Godot* has entertained audiences as diverse as children, prisoners and university students, and has been accepted as one of the classics of the twentieth-century stage.

Of course, it has never been without its critics. Norman Mailer characterized its admirers as "snobs of undue ambition and impotent imagination." And Beckett himself, called it a "bad" play.

Clearly, Samuel Beckett is not a writer for the general public. His work is for students and scholars. They have created an abundance of literature of their own about Beckett, including *The Journal of Beckett Studies*, begun in 1976.

In 1988, however, both general public and scholar alike competed for tickets to a performance of *Waiting for Godot* at Lincoln Center, in New York City. Directed by Mike Nichols and starring Robin Williams and Steve Martin, it received enormous publicity. Most noteworthy was the fact that the audience included the extremes of Beckett followers, including those who sat with annotated texts, monitoring every word and every action.

While it may be helpful to examine the roots of Beckett's work, it is also necessary to mention that a new category was invented by critics of the sixties. This category, Theater of the Absurd, was used to describe the new kind of theater that Beckett represented. Martin Esslin defined it as dealing with "its sense of the senselessness of the human condition and the inadequacy of the rational approach by the open abandonment of rational devices and discursive thought." It was characterized by absurd dialogue, characters and situations. It included the plays of Eugene Ionesco, Jean Genet, Harold Pinter and Edward Albee.

Beckett resisted the impulse to explain or categorize this material. In fact, he abhorred all attempts to do so. He wanted form and content to remain inseparable, and the reading or experience of the play to speak for itself.

Master List of Characters

Estragon (Gogo)—*Male vagabond in his later life; once a poet. Now ragged, with smelly and sore feet; longtime companion and friend of Vladimir.*

Vladimir (Didi)—*Male vagabond in later life; once respectable, now old and in pain, with garlic breath; possibly heavier than Estragon; more domineering and paternal.*

Lucky—*Obedient, male slave of Pozzo; with long, white hair; dances and thinks aloud on command in the first act; mute in the second act.*

Pozzo—*Sadistic, pipe smoking bald man who owns land and is a slave owner. Approximately in his sixties; intimidating voice; condescending attitude; in the first act, occasionally uses vaporizer for his throat and glasses for emphasis. Blind and helpless in the second act.*

A boy—*Timid and respectful. Of no particular age.*

Summary of the Play

Waiting for Godot is a play in two acts. Act I begins on a country road by a tree. It is evening. Estragon, an old man, is sitting on a low mound trying to remove his boot. Vladimir, another old man, joins him. They begin to chat.

They have apparently known each other for years. Once perhaps respectable, they are now homeless, debilitated, and often suicidal. They wonder out loud why they did not kill themselves years ago; they consider the possibility of doing it today. They are waiting for someone they call "Godot". While they wait, they share conversation, food, and memories.

Two other elderly men, Pozzo and Lucky, arrive on the scene. It is clear that Pozzo is the master, and Lucky is the slave. Upon command, the slave dances and thinks out loud for the entertainment of the others, until he is forcibly silenced.

After Lucky and Pozzo depart, a boy arrives. He tells Estragon and Vladimir that Godot will not be there today, but will be there tomorrow. He leaves, and they continue to wait.

The second act is almost the same as the first. The tree has sprouted leaves, Estragon and Vladimir chat while they wait for Godot, and Pozzo and Lucky arrive again. This time, Pozzo is blind and helpless, and Lucky is mute.

After some interaction, Pozzo and Lucky leave, and the boy arrives. He has the same message as before. Godot will be there tomorrow. Estragon and Vladimir are left to wait as before.

Estimated Reading Time

The play is in two acts, and it is about 100 pages long. The entire play can be read in less than two hours. The material requires more than one reading, and students should be patient with themselves and their ability to absorb its meaning. This is not an easy play; scholars have been dissecting it for years.

It is suggested that the play be read straight through the first time, in order to get a sense of the characters, the dialogue, and the concentric action.

Although it can be read silently, it may be helpful to stop at various points and read sections out loud. This will breathe life into the characters and center attention on the sound of the language. The monologues lend themselves to this kind of reading, but students should select sections based on their individual preferences, learning styles and background knowledge. If possible, students should work cooperatively with others and participate in a series of oral readings.

Videotapes and audiotapes are available at public libraries for various productions of *Waiting for Godot*. It is strongly suggested that the student make use of these additional resources.

This MAXnotes study guide is based on the Third Printing, 1978, by Grove Press, of *The Collected Works of Samuel Beckett — Waiting for Godot*.

The subdivisions for Act I (A-1 to A-6) and Act II (B-1 to B-5) are based on the *Regiebuch*, a detailed director's prompt book, written by Samuel Beckett as Director of the 1975 German production of *Warten auf Godot*.

In 1975, Samuel Beckett directed the German production, *Warten auf Godot*, at the Schiller Theater. For this occasion, "To give form to the confusion," he divided the play into eleven sections. These divisions served as a guide to the play's structure.

The format of this MAXnotes guide follows Beckett's outline. His *Regiebuch*, the guide for the German production, divides the play into the following sections:

A-1: Opening of Act I to "People are bloody ignorant apes."

A-2: Estragon's inspection ("Rises painfully...") to entry of Pozzo and Lucky.

A-3: The entrance of Pozzo and Lucky until Pozzo sits.

A-4: From Pozzo sitting down to Pozzo: "My memory is defective."

A-5: Estragon: "In the meantime nothing happens." to the exit of Pozzo and Lucky.

A-6: Exit of Pozzo and Lucky to end of Act I.

B-1: Opening of Act II to Vladimir: "Ah! Que voulez-vous. Exactly."

B-2: Estragon: "That wasn't such a bad little canter." to the entry of Pozzo and Lucky.

B-3: Entry of Pozzo and Lucky to Vladimir: "We are men."

B-4: Estragon: "Sweet mother earth!" to exit of Pozzo and Lucky.

B-5: Exit of Pozzo and Lucky to end of Act II.

SECTION TWO

Act I

Act I, Section A-1

New Characters:

Estragon: (Gogo): *half tramp, half clown, ex-poet, well over 50 years old; has sore feet, limps*

Vladimir (Didi): *once respectable friend of Gogo's; protective but domineering; walks with short stiff strides and legs apart; has bladder pain*

Summary

The play opens on a country road with a bare tree. It is evening. Estragon is sitting on a low mound, trying to remove his boot. "Nothing to be done," he says, as Vladimir approaches.

They greet each other as before. They have been apart, at least for the night, and Estragon tells of having been beaten by strangers in a ditch. Vladimir reminds himself of the burden of caring for Estragon. Suicide seems like a better idea. He laments not having done it years ago with Estragon, hand-in-hand from the top of the Eiffel Tower. Now it is too late. They are no longer respectable. They would not even be allowed to go up to the top of the Eiffel Tower.

Estragon asks for help with his boot, but gets none. Vladimir has his own problems; he has even forgotten to button his fly.

Estragon succeeds in removing his boot, and examines it. Vladimir removes his hat, and Estragon does the same. Vladimir suggests repenting. "Our being born?" Estragon says. Vladimir's laugh makes him grab himself in pain. He can't laugh, because he has too much physical pain. A smile will suffice.

Vladimir remembers a tale from the Bible, while Estragon re-members the maps from the Bible. The men have their own thoughts. When Vladimir questions the judgement of "Everybody," Estragon concludes, "People are bloody ignorant apes."

Analysis

Section A-1 establishes that there is "nothing to be done." It associates Estragon with boots and stone, and Vladimir with a hat and a tree. It introduces the theme of suicide and the "two thieves."

A-1 opens on a barren stage with a mound and a tree. This minimalistic landscape immediately invokes the theme of emptiness or nothingness, referred to by some critics as "the void." The play could be happening anywhere, at any time, although one of the critics noted that it seems to take place in the mountains of Dublin, at the lonely summit of Glencree, with its occasional threatened tree.

Estragon and Vladimir are tramps or vagabonds. They may belong to the category of people in Paris known as "clochards," who have known better times and have originally been cultured and educated. When Vladimir suggests, "you should have been a poet," Estragon tells him, "I was." In a conversation with one of his critics, Beckett was told that, at times, Estragon and Vladimir sound like they have earned advanced degrees. "How do you know they hadn't?" Beckett replied. Clearly homeless, they may also represent the rootless Anglo-Irish middle class in Ireland, who were neither English nor Irish, and were caught between two cultures in a politically charged environment.

Estragon spends a great deal of time trying to remove his boot. The stage directions read "He gives up, exhausted, rests, tries again. As before." During this period, there is no dialogue, and nothing much happens. This occurs throughout the play. Often, the directions read "silence" and "pause," marking important themes of waiting and nothingness.

"If they did it my way, they would empty the theatre," Beckett said. He wanted the audience to experience the agony of waiting, right along with the characters. Such is the essence of the play. The play is an event to be experienced; everyone waits, while nothing happens. One of Beckett's working titles was *En attendant*, which can be translated simply as "while waiting."

After the elapsed time, Estragon states, "Nothing to be done." This sentence is key to the rest of the play. It is a world in which nothing happens and nothing can be done.

Vladimir and Estragon talk to themselves before they talk to each other. For a brief moment they are separate individuals who come together to form two halves of a couple. One of their functions is to verify the existence of the other. "So there you are again," Vladimir says. "Am I?" Estragon wants to know.

Estragon, sitting on his mound, "is on the ground, he belongs to the stone," Beckett said. "Vladimir is light, he is oriented towards

the sky. He belongs to the tree." The stone and the tree are visual symbols for the pair.

This seems to tie in philosophically with the division of body and mind, earth and sky. In this first section, Estragon seems more grounded in his body and more of a concrete thinker. He needs to sit; he has trouble with his boot and his feet. Vladimir seems more mobile, more philosophical; he needs to stand; he has trouble with his hat. Vladimir's memory of the Bible is a literary image; Estragon's has a visual image.

The relationship of Estragon and Vladimir is outlined from the beginning. Although they are different, they seem to understand each other and depend on each other. They remain outside of each other's pain, but they play with its effects. Their antics have been compared to those of the Hollywood comedy team, Stan Laurel and Oliver Hardy. Beckett was a fan of theirs, and could easily have lifted the hat and boot routines from their movies.

The two men entertain themselves with their use of language. They welcome each other; they reminisce; they joke; they complain; they question each other; they tell stories; they scold each other. Their dialogue is a game. At one point, Vladimir pauses and says, "Come on, Gogo, return the ball," as if he and Estragon were rallying on the beloved tennis court of Beckett's youth.

The tale Vladimir remembers of the four evangelists and the two thieves creates a thread of insecurity. If, in this myth, only one of the four remembers that Christ saved a sinner who was crucified with him, although all four were there, is there any truth to the story? How does one know what to believe?

The reference to the "Two thieves, crucified at the same time as our Savior," brings up the much-debated question of the significance of religion in the play. The story of the Gospels, as relayed by Vladimir, refers to the works of St. Augustine, although the exact source is not clear. Beckett quoted it as, "Do not despair; one of the thieves was saved. Do not presume one of the thieves was damned." He used the theme of the two thieves throughout his play.

"I am aware of Christian mythology," Beckett said. "I have had the Bible read to me as a child, and have read the writing of others

who were affected by it and who used it in one form or another. Like all literary devices, I use it where it suites me. But to say I have been deeply affected by it … is utter nonsense."

He also noted, "My mother and brother got no value from their religion when they died. At the moment of crisis it had no more depth than an old school tie." Clearly, *Godot*, is not a religious play. The reference is a literary one, not a religious one.

Study Questions

1. When and where does this play take place?

2. Describe Estragon.

3. Describe Vladimir.

4. How are the men alike? How are they different?

5. Where did Estragon spend the night? What happened to him there?

6. What method of suicide does Vladimir suggest? Why wouldn't it work?

7. Why does Vladimir stop himself from laughing?

8. Vladimir and Estragon remember two different parts of the Gospels. Describe each one.

9. What is the matter with Estragon's foot?

10. "Nothing to be done" is repeated two times in this section. In each case, who says it and why?

Answers

1. The play takes place in the evening, on a country road by a tree.

2. Estragon was once a poet, and is dressed in rags and boots. He has sore feet and he limps. He is lighter than Vladimir.

3. Vladimir walks stiffly, with his legs apart. He has trouble with his bladder, and is in pain. He is wearing a hat.

4. The men are about the same age and from similar backgrounds. They seem to be in the same financial straits. Estragon seems more vulnerable and less practical than Vladimir.

5. Estragon spent the night in a ditch, where he was beaten by strangers.

6. Vladimir contemplates jumping down from the Eiffel Tower, hand-in-hand with Estragon. While it might have worked

years ago, now they would not be allowed to go up to the top of the tower.

7. Vladimir has pain when he laughs, because of his bladder.

8. Vladimir remembers the story of the two thieves who were crucified at the same time as Jesus. One was supposed to have been saved, and the other one damned. Estragon remembers the maps of the Holy Land.

9.   His foot is swollen and sore. His boot doesn't fit.

10. Estragon says it about his boot. Vladimir says it about his hat.

Suggested Essay Topics

1.   Estragon opens the play with the statement: "Nothing to be done." What supports that statement in this section? What contradicts it?

2.   What is the status of these men in society? How does Beckett convey this?

Act I, Section A-2

Summary

Estragon gets up from the mound. He is in pain. He limps around and wants to leave. Vladimir reminds him that they must stay and wait for Godot. Estragon is not sure that they are waiting in the right spot or on the right day. Vladimir examines the spot, points out the tree as the landmark, but gets confused about the day.

Estragon naps on the mound. Vladimir paces, then wakes him. "I felt lonely," Vladimir says. Estragon wants to share his dream, but Vladimir resists. They argue, then embrace.

The idea of suicide seems to appeal to both of them. They chat about the possibility of hanging themselves from the tree. "It'd give us an erection," Vladimir says. "Let's hang ourselves immediately!" Estragon concludes.

However, the method is problematic. The tree may not sustain Vladimir's weight, and he may be left all alone. Also, the possibility exists that Godot may come and offer them something they want, something they may have asked for. And so they wait.

When Estragon gets hungry, Vladimir produces a carrot. This leads to talk about food, then more talk about Godot. Estragon wants to know if they are "tied" to Godot. "Tied?" Vladimir asks. "Ti-ed." Estragon repeats. "But to whom? By whom?" Vladimir asks. "To your man," answers Estragon, who by this time seems to have forgotten Godot's name.

This discussion ends. Estragon repeats, "Nothing to be done," and offers the remainder of his carrot to Vladimir. At this moment, they hear "a terrible cry, close at hand." They huddle, cringe, and wait.

Analysis

In A-2, the waiting takes on a more active form. Estragon and Vladimir move around. They inspect the environment. They eat, they walk, and they consider suicide by hanging themselves from the tree.

This section introduces the character who is known as Godot. He is a person at this point. He has instructed the men to wait for him by the tree. He has a family, agents, and a bank account. It is only later in the play that Godot becomes a concept. He remains unseen and unknown.

For years, scholars have been debating the significance of the name, Godot. As usual, Beckett was no help in offering explanations. "If I knew I would have said so in the play," he has been quoted as saying

The English-speaking audience immediately connected it to the word "God," which was soon dismissed by the fact that the play was originally written in French. In every language, however, Beckett insisted that Godot be pronounced, "God-oh," with the accent on the first syllable, which reopens that particular debate.

For some reason, even though it was out of character, Beckett entertained all kinds of theories from critics about the nature of Godot. As late as 1972, he was saying that he "wanted any number of stories to be circulated," and "the more there are the better I like it." So, at various times, by various critics, it was suggested that Godot might be Happiness, Eternal Life, Love, Death, Silence, Hope, De Gaulle, Pozzo, a Balzac character, a bicycle racer, Time Future, a Paris street for call-girls, and a diminutive God ('ot' meaning 'little' in French).

Section A-2 begins with Estragon getting up and limping around. It ends with him saying, "Nothing to be done." This is the fourth repetition of this sentence in the play. There is nothing to be done about Estragon's boot, about Vladimir's hat or his physical

infirmity, and about their individual character traits. By this time, it is evident that repetition of language is a pattern in the play.

Ruby Cohn, a Beckett scholar, invented her own terminology for the verbal repetitions in *Waiting for Godot*:

simple doublet—when a word or phrase is heard again immediately or very soon after it is first mentioned; In A-1, Vladimir says "appalled" then "AP-PALLED.

interrupted doublet—when another speaker interrupts the original speaker who is repeating a phrase In A-1, the following exchange happens:

Vladimir: Imbecile! From death.
Estragon: I thought you said hell.
Vladimir: From death, from death.

distanced doubled—when a repetition is delayed too long to be readily recognized

echo doublet—when phrases are repeated by different characters. In A-1, it is placed here:

Estragon: In a ditch.
Vladimir: A ditch!

triplet—when a word or phrase is repeated three times; In A-1, it happens here:

Vladimir: It hurts?
Estragon: Hurts! He wants to know if it hurts.

multiplets—when words are repeated many times

a pounder—when multiplets spoken by a single character

a volley—when multiplets are echoed by one or more speakers

the refrain—a meaningful word or words often repeated during the course of a play, so that the audience becomes aware of the repetition; In A-1 and A-2, there is the statement, "Nothing to be done."

repeated negatives—words such as "nothing," "not," and phrases such as "I don't know"; the French particle "ne" was used about 513 times in the play.

Using "multiples" ending in a "volley" of the word "tied," Beckett manipulates the dialogue at the end of A-2 to anticipate the arrival of Pozzo and Lucky:

Estragon: We're not tied?
Vladimir: I don't hear a word you're saying.
Estragon: I'm asking you if we're tied.
Vladimir: Tied?
Estragon: Ti-ed.

Vladimir: How do you mean tied?
Estragon: Down.
Vladimir: But to whom? By whom?
Estragon: To your man.
Vladimir: To Godot? Tied to Godot! What an idea!

This "idea" creates the tension these characters feel through-out the play. Hopelessly adrift, they live on the verge of a constant unknown whose vague and various sounds bring them either hope or terror. This section ends with them "Huddled together, cringing away from the menace." And so, they wait.

Study Questions

1. Who are Vladimir and Estragon waiting for? Why?
2. Where does Estragon think the men were yesterday?
3. What are the nicknames of the characters?
4. Why does Estragon pull away from Vladimir when they embrace?
5. Why does Estragon want to hang himself "immediately?"
6. Why won't Estragon and Vladimir hang themselves?
7. What will Godot have to do before he promises them anything?
8. What food does Vladimir have in his pocket?
9. What is the difference in the way Estragon and Vladimir approach food?
10. Estragon repeats "Nothing to be done." Why?

Answers

1. They are waiting for someone named Godot, because he told them to wait for him. They hope he will help them in some way.
2. Estragon thinks they were exactly in the same place yesterday.
3. Estragon is called Gogo; Vladimir is called Didi.
4. Estragon pulls away because Vladimir has bad breath from the garlic he eats.
5. Estragon wants to hang himself because Vladimir suggests it would give him an erection.
6. There isn't any way they could hang themselves without one of the men remaining alive.
7. Godot will have to consult with his family, friends, agents, correspondents, books, and bank account.
8. Vladimir has turnips and a carrot in his pocket.

9. Estragon thinks the more food he eats, the worse it tastes. Vladimir feels the more he eats, the better it gets.

10. There is nothing to be done about his or Estragon's essential character.

Suggested Essay Topics

1. How does Beckett use language to define his characters and their relationship to each other?

2. Who does Godot seem to be at this point in the play? What could he possibly offer Estragon and Vladimir to improve their lives? Is there any suggestion that he might not appear?

Act I, Section A-3

New Characters:

Lucky: male, *looks very old and tired; has long gray hair and bulging eyes; his neck has running sores caused by the rope that is tied around it; once a great dancer and thinker, he now serves as Pozzo's slave; carries Pozzo's things and responds to his commands; has a temper that he uses against Estragon, and cries easily*

Pozzo: *gentleman landowner; bald and old; commanding presence; sadistic owner of Lucky; occasionally wears glasses, smokes a pipe*

Summary

Lucky enters with a rope around his neck. He is carrying "a heavy bag, a folding stool, a picnic basket and a greatcoat." Behind him, jerking the end of the long rope, is Pozzo. He is cracking a whip and yelling out commands.

At first, Estragon thinks this may be Godot. However, in a "terrifying voice," Pozzo introduces himself. He seems surprised that Estragon and Vladimir do not know of him. He puts on his glasses to make sure they "are human."

Pozzo inquires about Godot. This is Pozzo's land, although he admits, "The road is free to all", he wants to know why Estragon and Vladimir are there.

Almost immediately, however, he loses interest. He has his own business to attend to. Referring to Lucky as "pig" and "hog," he orders him to give him his coat, hold the whip, and open the stool so he can sit.

Lucky does as he is told, moving back and forth from his original spot. In between commands, he lifts the remaining baggage and stands motionless.

Pozzo sits down.

Analysis

This section introduces the second couple, Pozzo and Lucky, who are caricatures of the archetypical Master-Slave relationship from *Phenomenology of the Mind* by Hegel (1770-1831). It is the second pairing in the play, and provides a contrast to the relationship between Didi and Gogo. Each couple becomes more meaningful because of the other. When Pozzo and Lucky enter at the beginning of A-3, they are literally "tied" to each other with a rope. It is natural that Estragon assumes one of them is Godot, especially since Pozzo is pronounced "Pot-so," with the accent on the first syllable. Vladimir and Estragon play with his name for a bit, before concluding that he is not.

It is safe to assume that Beckett has carefully chosen the names of his characters. Estragon and Vladimir have eight letters and three syllables each. Their nicknames, Gogo and Didi, are both repetitive and childish, and have two letters and two syllables each. Pozzo and Lucky have five letters and two syllables each. Also, their names connote a European cross-section. Estragon is a French name; Vladimir is Russian; Pozzo is Italian; and Lucky is English.

Every word in this play is carefully chosen. Beckett exhibits a linguistic precision at all times, in all of his translations. The language is purposefully repetitive; there is not one wasted word or insignificant allusion in the play.

The psychological significance of these characters is open to debate. Some critics have said that the four figures represent four components of contemporary man. There is an inability to let go in all of them, even though they stagnate together. Pozzo, the pompous and tyrannical landlord, has the need to control. Lucky, his slave and victim, has the need to be protected. Vladimir remains impotent, though somewhat self-conscious: "I felt lonely." Estragon occasionally invokes the unconscious: "I had a dream."

By silent agreement, Pozzo and Lucky have entered into a sado-masochistic bondage. Vladimir and Estragon have the symbiotic love-hate relationship of some unhappy couples.

This was not Beckett's interpretation. Although he was well versed in the writings of Freud and Jung, he rarely engaged in this kind of psychobabble. When his actors asked for explanations, he gave them physical and visual images instead (Estragon's mound, Vladimir's tree, Pozzo's whip, Lucky's neck). However, he once commented that Pozzo was a weak character with the need to over-compensate.

The origins of the couple idea first appeared in Beckett's novel, *Le Voyage de Mercier et Camier,* which remained unpublished for a long time. Mercier may be representative of the mind, the Camier, the body. The similarities to Didi and Gogo are clear. Didi of Act I speaks as mind, and Gogo as body. Didi ponders spiritual salvation, while Gogo eats, sleeps, and is afraid of being beaten. This duality (referred to by Beckett as the "pseudocouple"), was said to have replaced the old protagonist and antagonist of dramatic tradition.

Study Questions

1. How are Vladimir and Estragon feeling when Lucky and Pozzo enter?

2. What are Vladimir and Estragon holding when they enter?

3. How does Pozzo describe Lucky when they arrive?

4. Who does Estragon think Pozzo is?

5. What other names do the men associate with the name "Pozzo?"

6. Why does Pozzo burst into "an enormous laugh?"

7. Why does Pozzo conclude that Estragon and Vladimir have the right to be on his property?

8. Why is Pozzo happy to see the two men?

9. Why can't Lucky hold the whip in his hand?

10. What possessions does Pozzo seem to be travelling with?

Answers

1. They are frightened, "huddled together, shoulders hunched, cringing away."

2. Pozzo is holding the end of a rope that is around Lucky's neck. Lucky is carrying a heavy load of baggage.

3. Pozzo says that Lucky is wicked with strangers.

4. Estragon thinks Pozzo is Godot.

5. Estragon thinks he is saying his name is "Booz." Vladimir remembers a family named "Gozzo."

6. Pozzo thinks it is funny that he Estragon and Vladimir can be classified as humans, like himself, "Made in God's image."

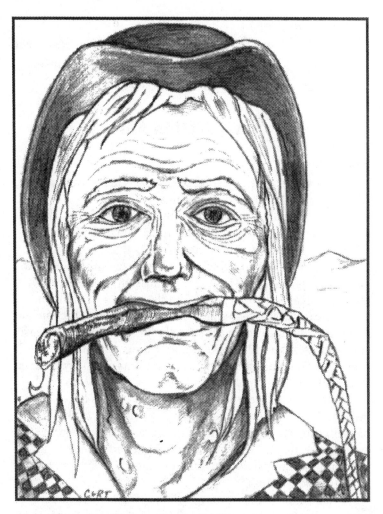

7. Pozzo says that while he owns the property, the road is public property.

8. He is happy to see them because he has been travelling for a long time without seeing anyone.

9. Lucky's hands are filled with the bag, basket, and stool.

10. Pozzo has a bag, basket, stool, coat, whip, glasses, watch, and slave.

Suggested Essay Topics

1. Describe Pozzo and Lucky and their relationship to each other.
2. Compare the relationship between Vladimir and Estragon to the relationship between Pozzo and Lucky.

Act I, Section A-4

Summary

Lucky goes back to his spot. Pozzo opens the basket, removes the chicken and wine, and starts eating.

Vladimir and Estragon takes a closer look at Lucky. They inspect his face and the sores on his neck. They wonder out loud whether he is "a halfwit" or "a cretin."

Estragon wants the chicken bones Pozzo's thrown on the ground. He is told to ask Lucky for permission to eat them. When Lucky ignores him, Pozzo grants him permission to eat them.

While Pozzo smokes his pipe, Vladimir and Estragon complain about the "disgrace" of Lucky's treatment. They decide to leave. However, Pozzo reminds them about their appointment with Godot. He does not want them to go; he wants company while he smokes his second pipe.

Estragon and Vladimir wonder why Lucky does not put down his bags. They ask Pozzo about this, but he is too busy talking about himself. They ask again. This time, Pozzo relishes the attention ("Is everybody listening? Is everybody ready?"), and even jerks Lucky to attention. However, by the time he is ready to answer, he has forgotten the question.

When it is repeated, Pozzo goes into a lengthy explanation. He explains that he is on his way to sell Lucky at the fair. Since Lucky does not want to be sold, he is trying to impress Pozzo with his actions.

At this point, Lucky starts crying. Pozzo gives Estragon a handkerchief to wipe away the tears. As Estragon attempts this, Lucky kicks him in the shin, drawing blood.

Vladimir is horrified at Pozzo's insensitivity. As soon as his pain subsides, Estragon joins Vladimir in reprimanding Pozzo. They go

on until Pozzo gives up sobbing. "He used to be so kind...so help-ful...and entertaining...my good angel...and now...he's killing me."

However, Pozzo forgets his moment of weakness almost immediately. He starts rummaging for his pipe, to Estragon's delight, until Vladimir has to run offstage to relieve himself.

Upon his return, the three men look up at the sky, discuss the appointment with Godot, fiddle with their belongings, and gener-ally relax with each other. Pozzo asks for some reassurance as to his character. Once he gets it, he admits that he has "need of encouragement," and that his "memory is defective."

Analysis

A-4 focuses on Pozzo's discourse as he attempts to impress Vladimir and Estragon. For the moment, Didi and Gogo are entertained during their waiting period. Pozzo and Lucky become a so-called "play within a play." They create a diversion for Estragon and Vladimir, who then let the audience know that they are aware of being present at their own spectacle.

> Vladimir: Charming evening we're having.
> Estragon: Unforgettable.
> Vladimir: And it's not over.
> Estragon: Apparently not.
> Vladimir: It's only beginning.
> Estragon: It's awful.
> Vladimir: Worse than the pantomine.
> Estragon: The circus.
> Vladimir: The music-hall.
> Estragon: The circus.

When Vladimir 'hastens towards the wings,' Estragon calls after him, "End of the corridor, on the left," and he answers, "Keep my seat." In this exchange, Beckett has temporarily broken the "fourth wall," a term given to the invisible wall that separates the audience from the actors on stage. Estragon and Vladimir are now spectators.

"Why doesn't he put down his bags?", Estragon says about Lucky. This will be repeated as the play unfolds, and become a refrain. In this section, Lucky is never free of his load. His repetitive gestures with Pozzo's belongings define his character. On command, he lifts and replaces the stool, the basket, and the coat.

A close examination of Lucky's physical appearance reveals the distortions created by a life of servitude. Pozzo might be Lucky's Godot, but the result is a debilitated and deformed human specimen.

Estragon approaches Lucky by addressing him as "Mister," then again "Mister." The language of the "double mister" is right from the Dublin streets. Beckett takes some of his language from Irish colloquialisms, as did James Joyce in *Ulysses:* "Eh, Mister! Your fly is open, Mister."

At long last, Vladimir gives a sense of his humanitarian feeling by saying, "It's a scandal...! To treat a man...like that...I think that...no...a human being...no...it's a scandal!" Estragon, more involved with his eating, chimes in with "A disgrace!" The two of them get back to the business of their own physical selves, however, when Lucky kicks Estragon in his shin.

There is a vast difference between the couples Lucky and Pozzo, and Estragon and Vladimir. The former pair is goal directed. They have a destination and a plan. They have a past and a future. The latter have no plan, no goal, no destination. They can either wait for Godot or not. However, the only alternative to waiting seems to be death.

Pozzo tries to impress Estragon and Vladimir with his possessions. He makes a huge ordeal of his basket of food and wine, his vaporizer to clear his throat, his watch, and his pipe. "I've lost my Kapp and Peterson!" he cries, referring to the briar he purchased at one of Dublin's finest pipe shops.

He then tries to impress them with poetic language, and goes off into a soliloquy about the sky. "What is there so extraordinary about it. Qua sky. It is pale and luminous like any sky at this hour of the day. In these latitudes...."

At the end, he asks: "How did you find me?" Estragon's response, "Oh tray bong, tray tray tray bong," is again lifted from Dublin street conversation, where humor was derived from exaggerating well-known French sayings. Pozzo's need for this kind of reassurance leads him to admit to some weakness in his character. He explains it by saying, "You see my memory is defective."

Study Questions

1. Once seated, what does Pozzo do?
2. What are Lucky's physical characteristics?

38   *Waiting for Godot*

3. What does Pozzo do after he eats?

4. What does Estragon want from Pozzo?

5. What does Vladimir think about Pozzo's treatment of Lucky?

6. Why does Pozzo want to meet Godot?

7. Why doesn't Lucky put down his bags?

8. Why does Pozzo want to get rid of Lucky?

9. Who cries in this section and why?

10. Why does Pozzo think the sky is so extraordinary?

Answers

1. Once seated, Pozzo drinks his wine and eats his chicken.

2. Lucky has a running sore on his neck. He is good looking, but effeminate. He drools, and his eyes bulge.

3. After he eats, Pozzo smokes his pipe.

4. Estragon wants the bones from Pozzo's chicken.

5. Vladimir thinks that the way Pozzo treats Lucky is scandalous.

6. Pozzo wants to meet Godot, because he feels the more people he meets, the happier he becomes.

7. Lucky doesn't put down his bags because he wants to impress Pozzo with the amount of work he can do. He doesn't want Pozzo to get rid of him.

8. Pozzo wants to sell Lucky at the fair for money. He is no longer worth anything to him. Instead of kicking Lucky out, he wants to offer Lucky up for sale.

9. Lucky cries because he does not want to be sold. Estragon cries out in pain because Lucky kicks him in the shin. Pozzo cries because of his good memories of Lucky.

10. Pozzo thinks the sky is extraordinary because of the way it changes color throughout the day. He also is impressed with the way it suddenly changes to create night.

Suggested Essay Topics

1. Does Pozzo's character change during this section of the play? Does he seem to be the same character who entered at the beginning of Section A-3?

2. What evidence is there, in this section, that Pozzo and Lucky become part of a "play within a play?"

Act I, Section A-5

Summary

Pozzo wants to repay Estragon and Vladimir for being "civil" to him. Although Estragon suggests money, Pozzo offers entertainment.

He proposes that Lucky dance, sing, recite, or think for them. Estragon suggests that Lucky first dance, then think. On command, Lucky puts down his bags and dances the same step twice.

Although this attempt proves disappointing, Vladimir wants to hear Lucky think. Pozzo insists that Vladimir return Lucky's hat to his head in order to get him to perform. Once this task is accomplished, Pozzo commands, "Think, pig!"

Lucky does so. He shouts out a litany of remarks. At long last, Vladimir grabs his hat. Lucky falls and is finally silent.

Pozzo, in his anger, takes the hat, tramples it, and announces, "There's an end to his thinking!"

Worried that Lucky may now be dead, Vladimir and Estragon attempt to lift him and hold him up. They quickly grow impatient with this, and allow him to fall.

Upon Pozzo's insistence, they finally get him standing again on his own, holding the bags. Pozzo hunts for his watch, doesn't find it, realizes he must have left it at home, and attempts to go.

This is not an easy task. "I don't seem to be able…(long hesitation)…to depart." he says. "Such is life," Estragon agrees.

However, before long, Pozzo and Lucky exit.

Analysis

A-5 focuses on Lucky. He is built up by Pozzo as one who can perform any number of feats. Like any circus animal, he supposedly has the ability to dance, sing, recite, or even think on command.

However, his dance proves disappointing, and his "think" overwhelming. Naming the dance becomes a guessing game for

Estragon and Vladimir. In reality, giving it a name was kind of a game for Beckett. He toyed with the idea of naming it "the death of the duck," with duck meaning "joke" or "malicious lie," or "the death of the lamplighter," which referred to the lowliest employee in a French railway station, to whom death would be a relief. Estragon guesses the title to be "The Scapegoat's Agony," which also implies relief from suffering. Vladimir comes up with "The Hard Stool," which refers to constipation. Calling it "The Net," however, gives it the added dimension of interminable entanglement.

Lucky's speech follows this pathetic display. In its presentation and philosophy, it demonstrates human suffering and decline. It is perhaps the kind of verbiage that goes through the mind of those on the verge of death. Perhaps it is even what the dying say. Through Lucky's words and actions, disintegration takes on a human form.

Although some critics have dismissed it as gibberish, or as the "word-salad" of schizophrenics, the speech is actually a carefully constructed, three-part critique. The first section describes the idea of a diminishing personal god who is no longer feeling, moving, speaking ("divine apathia, divine athambia, divine aphasia"), ending with the line "but not so fast." The second section, starting with "considering what is more," is about man who is shrinking and dwindling ("wastes and pines wastes and pines"). The third section fixes on "the earth abode of stones," starting from the line "considering what is more, much more grave."

Lucky's speech or "tirade" is filled with the kind of verbal repetitions defined by Ruby Cohn. "Simple doublets" can be seen in the repetition of "for reasons unknown but time will tell," and "winter winter." "Multiplets" that form "pounders" can be seen in "in spite of the tennis," "I resume," and "alas."

Some of the language Lucky uses is there just for effect, to create a mood of confusion and horror. At the same time, some of it refers to Beckett's own derisive humor, game playing, philosophy, and environment.

"Acacacacademy of Anthropopopometry of Essy-in-Possy" mocks academia. "Fartov," Beckett quipped, meant "to fart," and

"Belcher," "to belch." "Camogie" is an Irish game. Bishop Berkeley, the Bishop of Cloyne, was an eighteenth-century educator and philosopher who believed that existence was dependent on perception. "Connemara" is a western section of Galway known for its colorful landscape of mountains, lakes and the Atlantic shoreline. By the end, the speech deteriorates into repetitions and isolated words—"tennis... the stones... so calm... Cunard... unfinished..."—and Lucky has to be forcibly silenced.

The monologue summarizes the position of the two tramps, Lucky, his master and all people, who are condemned to age and die on earth. Having relayed this message, Lucky collapses. He is kicked by Pozzo, and lifted by Vladimir and Estragon. He finally resumes his position as an obedient slave. Though he "totters, reels sags," with help he remains "on his feet, bag and basket in his hands."

The language takes on the quality of Ruby Cohn's "volleys" with repetitions of "adieu," "yes," "no," and "on" as A-5 ends.

Study Questions

1. How does Estragon want Pozzo to repay him for being "civil" to him?

2. What does Pozzo suggest as repayment?

3. What does Estragon want Lucky to do? What does Vladimir want Lucky to do?

4. What is Estragon's reaction to Lucky's dance?

5. What is the name of Lucky's dance? Why does he call it that?

6. Why did Lucky finally put down his bags?

7. Before Lucky thinks, what does he need?

8. How do Estragon, Vladimir, and Pozzo react to Lucky's speech?

9. How do they get him to stop?

10. At the end of this section, what has Pozzo misplaced? Where does he think it may be?

Answers

1. Estragon wants Pozzo to repay him with money; first ten francs, then five.

2. Pozzo suggests that he have Lucky perform for them, either dance, or sing, or think, or recite.

3. Estragon wants Lucky to dance; Vladimir wants Lucky to think.

4. Estragon is disappointed in the dance; he thinks he can do as well. He tries, but fails.

5. Lucky calls the dance, "The Net," because he thinks of himself entangled in a net.

6. He put down his bags in order to dance.

7. Before he can think, he needs to have his hat on his head.

8. All three men get more and more agitated during Lucky's speech. They all try to get him to stop.

9. At long last, they get him to stop by removing his hat.

10. Pozzo can't find his watch or half-hunter that his Grandfather gave him. He thinks he left it at home.

Suggested Essay Topics

1. Estragon wants Lucky to dance; Vladimir wants him to think. How do their choices fit in with their general characters?

2. Lucky's speech has been called gibberish or the "word-salad" of schizophrenics. What elements of it make sense?

Act I, Section A-6

New Character:

Boy: *delivers messages for Godot and takes care of his goats; somewhat fearful and shy*

Summary

Estragon wants to leave. Vladimir reminds him that they must wait for Godot. A boy arrives with a message from Godot. Before he has a chance to continue, Estragon grabs him and shakes him. Vladimir intervenes.

Estragon admits that he is "unhappy," but doesn't remember why. He manages to limp to his mound, sit down, and remove his boots.

Finally, the boy blurts out the message. "He tells them that Godot will not come this evening but surely tomorrow."

Vladimir questions the boy about his job, his brother, and his relationship with Godot. The boy tells him that he takes care of Godot's goats while his brother "minds the sheep." Godot is good to him, but beats his brother. The boy asks what he should tell Godot. "Tell him you saw us," Vladimir replies.

The boy runs off. It is night. The moon rises. Estragon leaves his boots on the ground, for someone with "smaller feet." He wants to go barefoot, like Christ.

Vladimir assures Estragon that "Tomorrow will be better;" Godot will be there. Estragon wants to bring rope to hang himself. He reminisces about a former suicide attempt.

They consider the possibility of parting, but they stay together. They agree to leave, but they do not move.

Analysis

A-6 is the exchange with the boy, and the fall of night. It begins after a long "silence," after which Vladimir notes, "That passed the time." Three themes are again called into play: the theme of silence and pause; the theme of "What do we do now?"; and the theme of "We're waiting for Godot." These are the themes of the play as well as the refrains or leitmotifs. One critic concluded that the entire plot of this play can be summarized in four words: "We're waiting for Godot."

After a brief exchange, during which Vladimir reminds Estragon of the events that just occurred and seem to have occurred before, the boy arrives. This is Godot's messenger, and he is presented as one of two brothers. Even he is half of a couple.

He delivers the same monotonous message, the one they have heard before. The moon rises as the boy exits. The rising moon is a perfect circle, bringing the day to a close. The day is ending; there is a theme of completion. Godot has not arrived; there is a theme of incompletion. Vladimir says: "At last," as if relieved. Estragon attempts a poetic reference, and then compares himself to a suffering and "barefoot" Christ as he removes his boots.

Study Questions

1. How does Vladimir sum up Lucky and Pozzo's visit?

2. Why does Vladimir think he knows the visitors?

3. Why does Estragon "hobble?"

4. Who enters next?

5. What does he want?

6. Why did he hesitate before speaking up?

7. How is Estragon feeling at this point in the play?

8.   What does the boy say about himself?

9.   What does Estragon do with his boots? Why?

10.   Why does Estragon compare himself to Christ?

Answers

1.   Vladimir says it helped pass the time.

2.   Vladimir thinks that he has seen Pozzo and Lucky before. He thinks they have changed from the last time he saw them.

3.   Estragon is having trouble with both of his feet now.

4.   A boy enters.

5.   The boy wants to give them a message from Godot. Godot will not be there today. He will arrive tomorrow.

6.   He hesitated because he was afraid of Lucky and Pozzo. He was afraid of the whip and the roars.

7.   Estragon says he is unhappy.

8.   The boy says he works for Godot, as a goatherd, and has a brother, who works as a shepherd. His brother gets beaten by Godot, but he doesn't.

9.   Estragon takes off his boots, and leaves them on the ground. He hopes someone with smaller feet will find them and wear them.

10.   Estragon thinks he is like Christ because he too walks barefoot. He says he always compares himself to Christ.

Suggested Essay Topics

1.   How does the theme of "silence" tie in with the theme of "waiting" in this section?

2.   By the end of this section, there is evidence of the "pseudo-couple" or pairing of characters in Vladimir and Estragon, Pozzo and Lucky, and the boy and Godot. Describe and contrast each couple.

SECTION THREE

Act II

Act II, Section B-1

Summary

It is the next day, the same time, the same place. Estragon's boots are where he left them, "heels together, toes splayed." The tree has a few leaves.

Vladimir enters and sings a song. Estragon arrives, barefoot and unhappy. They greet each other and embrace. Vladimir's singing made Estragon feel unwanted. "He's all alone, he thinks I'm gone forever, and he sings."

Vladimir tries to explain his mood, but can't. Estragon's been beaten again, this time by "ten of them." Vladimir is reminded of Estragon's dependence on him. They agree to say to each other, "We are happy."

Vladimir remembers "yesterday," the tree, Pozzo and Lucky, the scenery. Estragon has forgotten the tree. He remembers getting kicked and eating bones. Vladimir talks of the Macon country, of picking grapes with Estragon, some time before. Estragon becomes angry. He doesn't remember that part of his life. He only knows where he is now—in the Cackon country.

They talk of the dead and death. They remember Godot. Again they wait. While they wait, they contradict each other and question each other. They manage to pass the time.

Analysis

B-1, like A-1, defines the situation. Vladimir and Estragon question the time and place of their appointment, and go through their verbal patter to pass the time.

The "round-song" that Vladimir sings while he "comes and goes" from the stage is from a German children's song. The words give the sense of an eternal refrain ("and dug the dog a tomb") which might go on forever. The repetition of the dialogue, starting from the greeting ("Come here until I embrace you", a Dublin colloquialism) also suggests a sort of ritual that might go on forever.

The song indicates the recurrent shape in *Godot*. "I take no sides. I am interested in the shape of ideas," Beckett once remarked. Like the song, the shape of this play is circular. The words and actions come back to the same starting place, only to begin again.

The only indication that time has passed comes from the tree. It has sprouted some leaves. otherwise, the two characters appear unchanged. The stage directions do not indicate costume changes for Estragon and Vladimir. However, in Beckett's *Regiebuch*, they have exchanged jackets and pants. They may be the same as before but have come to be more of a part of each other.

This section demonstrates further the relationship between Estragon and Vladimir. "Don't touch me! Don't question me! Don't speak to me! Stay with me!" Estragon demands. These mixed messages have been compared to the dynamic that exists between couples who have been together for a long period of time. As a matter of fact, Beckett's friends insisted that he had taken the dialogue straight from the repartée he had with his wife. Their relationship resembled that of two Irish "butties" exchanging vaudeville one-liners (cross-talk) in the old music-hall tradition. It is perhaps that image that best fits this play.

Vladimir and Estragon have different perceptions of time. Vladimir has a firm sense of "today" over yesterday, after a night spent alone but happy. Estragon claims not to know whether time actually passed. His mind has not retained the images of the tree and the attempted suicide or the appearance of Pozzo and Lucky.

Although the wait seems eternal, the act of waiting becomes more playful as well as more desperate. Vladimir and Estragon engage in a kind of dialogue that has been compared to the single lines of verse in Greek plays, called stichomythic play:

Vladimir: You're right, we're inexhaustible.
Estragon: It's so we won't think.
Vladimir: We have that excuse.
Estragon: It's so we won't hear.
Vladimir: We have our reasons.

Estragon: All the dead voices.
Vladimir: They make a noise like wings.
Estragon: Like leaves.
Vladimir: Like sand.
Estragon: Like leaves.

The words here are simple, idiomatic and rhythmic. The sparse poetic language fits together and produces a kind of haunting chant. All of it leads to the refrain:

Estragon: What do we do now?
Vladimir: Wait for Godot.
Estragon: Ah!

Study Questions

1. Where and when does Act II begin?

2. What does Vladimir do when he enters?

3. What is Vladimir's reaction to seeing Estragon?

4. What is Estragon's reaction to seeing Vladimir?

5. What happened to Estragon in the night?

6. What does Vladimir remember about the tree?

7. What does Estragon say about his memory?

8. What country does Estragon think they are in now? What country does Vladimir remember?

9. Why does Estragon think they need to keep talking?

10. Why are the two men there again?

Answers

1. Act II begins in the same place on the next day.

2. When Vladimir enters, he comes and goes on stage, examines the boots, and sings a song.

3. Vladimir seems happy to see Estragon and wants to hug him.

4. Estragon is angry at Vladimir. He is horrified that Vladimir seems so happy when the two of them are apart. He is upset that Vladimir left him alone.

5. Estragon was beaten again in the night by ten strangers.

6. He remembers that they wanted to hang themselves from it.

7. Either he forgets things immediately or he never forgets them.

8. Estragon thinks they have always been in the Cackon country. Vladimir remembers being with Estragon in the Macon country.

9. Estragon thinks they need to talk in order to keep from thinking and listening to their own sad memories.

10. They are there waiting for Godot.

Suggested Essay Topics

1. How does the theme of "circularity" define this section?

2. Compare and contrast the ways Vladimir and Estragon deal with "time" and the past.

Act II , Section B-2

Summary

Vladimir talks about what just occurred. He notices how the tree has changed. The tree was bare and black and now it is covered with leaves.

He tries to remind Estragon of the encounter with Pozzo and Lucky. He succeeds in finding Estragon's wound. Then he sees Estragon's boots. Estragon insists they are not his.

Estragon is tired and wants to leave. Vladimir reminds him about Godot.

This time, the only food in Vladimir's pocket is a black radish and turnips. He offers to go find carrots, but he does not move.

Vladimir puts the boots on Estragon's feet. They are loose but fit. Estragon sits on his mound and tries to sleep while Vladimir sings. At first, the singing is too loud. When it is softer, Estragon falls asleep.

When he awakens, he wants to tell his dream, but is silenced. Then he wants to leave. They can't because of Godot.

They find Lucky's hat. They play at exchanging and adjusting hats. Estragon wants to leave; Vladimir wants to play.

They play at being Lucky and Pozzo—Vladimir as Lucky; Estragon as Pozzo. They part, then come together again.

They fear someone is approaching. They try hiding behind the tree. The tree can't hide them. They are safe anyway because nobody comes.

They exchange insults, ending with Estragon's "Crritic!" They make up, do exercises, deep breathing, and play at being the tree.

Analysis

B-2, which opens with Estragon's "What do we do now?" parallels A-2 by presenting an assortment of activities to pass the time. Estragon eats radishes. Vladimir and Estragon walk about. Estragon sleeps while Vladimir sings him a lullaby. They exchange insults. They play Pozzo and Lucky, they do calisthenics; and they pass around the hats.

Although it is not evident in their physical appearance, the passage of time has had an effect on Estragon and Vladimir. Their word games are shorter, their actions are fewer, and their despair is greater. "We can always find something, eh Didi, to give us the impression that we exist?" Estragon says. The forgetful, and perhaps aging Vladimir, responds with - "...let us persevere in what we have resolved, before we forget."

As suicide was suggested in A-2, as something to do "while waiting," Estragon suggests that they abuse each other, and Vladimir suggests doing exercises. These are all language games, designed to pass the time. Whatever escape they provide is momentary; Estragon and Vladimir's condition is permanent. The tragedy of their situation is circular: it keeps returning to the same lack of purpose. All attempts at escape are illusory. In fact, they do not take action; they merely talk about it.

The fast exchanges of hats, taken directly from the vaudeville-style routines of Laurel and Hardy, brings a brief moment of humor. This juggling ends with Estragon wearing Lucky's hat. Perhaps he has inherited Lucky's tongue. This may anticipate Lucky's return in B-3, when he can no longer speak.

Study Questions

1. What does Vladimir notice about the tree?
2. What does Vladimir remember?
3. What does Estragon remember?
4. What does Estragon say about the boots?
5. What is different about the food Vladimir has in his pocket now compared with the food he had in A-2?
6. What is different about the boots?
7. How does Vladimir try to help Estragon get sleep?
8. What has Lucky left behind? What do they do with it?
9. Who plays Lucky? Who plays Pozzo?
10. What insults do they hurl at each other?

Answers

1. Vladimir notices that the tree, which seemed dead before, has grown leaves.
2. Vladimir remembers everything. He remembers the scenery and the exchange with Lucky and Pozzo.
3. Estragon remembers that he was kicked.
4. Estragon says that the boots are not his. He says his were black or a kind of gray, and these are brownish green.
5. Vladimir had edible food in his pocket in A-2; now all he has are turnips and one black radish.
6. The boots seem to fit Estragon now.
7. Vladimir sings Estragon a lullaby.

8. Lucky left his hat behind. Vladimir picks it up and puts it on his head. Then he and Estragon play a game of exchanging hats that ends with Vladimir wearing Lucky's hat.

9. Vladimir plays Lucky; Estragon plays Pozzo.

10. They call each other "Moron," "Vermin," "Abortion," "Morpion," "Sewer-rat," "Curate," and "Cretin."

Suggested Essay Topics

1. Describe the ways Vladimir and Estragon pass the time in this section.

2. What indications are there that time has passed? Have the characters changed in any way?

Act II, Section B-3

Summary

Pozzo and Lucky enter. Pozzo is now blind. Otherwise they seem the same. The rope is shorter than before and seems to be pulling Pozzo; the other trappings are the same. As they enter, Pozzo bumps into Lucky, and they both fall.

Vladimir recognizes Pozzo; Estragon thinks he is Godot. Although Pozzo asks for help again and again, his pleas are ignored.

Estragon and Vladimir discuss the situation. Vladimir philosophizes about this-and-that. Estragon concludes, "We are all born mad. Some remain so."

Pozzo offers to pay for help. Vladimir finally attempts to pull him up, but fails. Estragon threatens to leave. Someone farts. Estragon tries to help Vladimir up, but he also falls. They are all down on the ground. Pozzo asks "Who are you?" Vladimir replies, "We are men."

Analysis

B-3 is a reversal of A-4. Pozzo, who dominated Vladimir and Estragon with his chatter, is now on the ground crying for help, and it is Vladimir who dominates this section with his rhetoric.

Pozzo and Lucky have changed since Act I. Pozzo is blind and, although it is not apparent until B-4, Lucky is dumb. There are no outward changes in Vladimir and Estragon. They may be sentenced to life forever. They seem not to have aged, nor are they dead. Neither one, however, immediately recognizes Pozzo and Lucky. Vladimir then notices Pozzo, and reminds Estragon of the previous events.

Vladimir's use of terms such as "amuck" were taken right from the Dublin streets. In this section, he seems to be engaged in a conversation with himself that continues on despite numerous interruptions:

> Vladimir: We were beginning to weaken. Now we are sure to see the evening out.
> Pozzo: Help!
> Vladimir: We are no longer alone waiting for the night, waiting for Godot, waiting for...waiting. All evening we have struggled, unassisted. Now it's over. It's already tomorrow.
> Pozzo: Help.
> Vladimir: Time flows again already. The sun will set, the moon rise, and we away...from here.

Vladimir's lengthy speech is filled with metaphysical observations. "But at this place at this moment of time, all mankind is us, whether we like it or not." It is also filled with cliches. "But that is not the question. What are we doing here, that is the question." He temporarily ends it with, "We are waiting for Godot to come," adding, "Or for night to fall." Either one will do. This is why at the end of Act I, he seemed so relieved when he said, "At last."

This section ends with all four men down on the ground. Although they retain their individuality, they seem to be wrapped in a common fate—that of disintegration. Rather than having a climax or a peak, as did traditional drama, this play demonstrates an inexorable levelling down. Here it falls to a low point, or nadir. The characters are down, and they cannot get up.

Study Questions

1. What physical changes are apparent in Lucky and Pozzo?

2. What happens when they first enter?

3. What does Pozzo keep asking for?

4. Who does Estragon think it is?

5. What does Estragon want from Pozzo?

6. What two things does Vladimir suggest may occur?

7. How does Estragon summarize Vladimir's rhetoric?

8. How does Pozzo try to get the men to help him?

9. What happens when Vladimir tries to help Pozzo get up? What happens to Estragon when he tries to help Vladimir?

10. How are all four characters alike at the end of this section?

Answers

1. The rope that connects them is shorter. Lucky is wearing a different hat.

2. Lucky stops short upon seeing Vladimir and Estragon. Pozzo bumps into him, and they both fall.

3. Pozzo keeps asking for help.

4. Estragon again thinks he is Godot.

5. Estragon wants more food from Pozzo.

6. Vladimir suggests that either Godot will come or night will fall.

7. Estragon summarizes it as, "We are all born mad. Some remain so."

8. He offers them money.

9. Vladimir falls, then Estragon falls.

10. All four characters are men; all four characters are down on the ground.

Suggested Essay Topics

1. Compare the contrast Pozzo in A-3 with Pozzo in B-3.

2. How would critics justify that the play never reaches a "peak" but, rather, a "nadir." Include definitions of each term in your answer.

Act II, Section B-4

Summary

Pozzo crawls away but remains down. Vladimir, is afraid Pozzo is dying. Estragon responds by amusing himself. He calls Pozzo, "Abel," and Lucky, "Cain." Then he ponders a cloud.

Vladimir and Estragon decide to pass the time by helping Pozzo. Once up, Pozzo tells them he is blind. They carry him around for a while, then release him. Pozzo has lost his sense of time, and wants to locate Lucky. "Where is my menial?" he asks.

Vladimir suggests this is Estragon's chance to get back at Lucky for kicking him. Lucky is down, and Estragon can revive him by following Pozzo's suggestions of pulling the rope or giving him "a taste of his boot, in the face and the privates...."

Estragon starts kicking him. In the process, he hurts himself, retires to the mound, and falls asleep.

Pozzo commands Lucky to get up. When he is up, he lifts the bags, puts the end of his rope in Pozzo's hand, and they are ready to go.

Vladimir wants to hear Lucky sing or think or recite. "But he is dumb," Pozzo responds. "Since when?" Vladimir asks. Furious at his obsession with time, Pozzo blurts out, "One day, is that not enough for you, one day he went dumb, one day I went blind, one day we'll go deaf, one day we were born, one day we shall die, the same day, the same second.... They give birth astride of a grave, the light gleams an instant, then it's night once more." Pozzo pulls on the rope and he and Lucky leave.

Analysis

In B-4, the physical action centers on the four characters getting up after having fallen down. Pozzo and Lucky prepare for their exit. As in A-5, the action of B-4 focuses on Lucky, the classic victim. Kicked by Estragon, he resumes his tentatively upright position, loaded down with baggage. Lucky is now more impaired than before. After a reference to his ability to dance and speak, and a request by Vladimir for him to sing, Pozzo announces that he is dumb.

Originally, when Beckett created his *Regiebuch,* he wanted the movement of the actor playing Vladimir to imitate the circular rotation of the earth. When Pozzo, now blind, asks, "What's it like?" in an attempt to get his bearings, Vladimir was to begin to turn in a clockwise direction. After every line, he was to turn a quarter of the way around and stop. This was in keeping with Beckett's decision to have all lines in the play that referred to temporal concepts, those dealing with time in an earthly existence, accompanied by either clockwise or counter-clockwise motions of hands and feet. Clockwise motion represented lines about living in a temporal world and counter-clockwise motions indicated escape from that world.

This was in keeping with the instructions in the opening of the play. Here, the actor playing Estragon was instructed to make large, circular gestures with his hands while saying, "Nothing to be done." Although these gestures were outlined by Beckett, they were not always performed as written. However, Beckett clearly wanted to convey the theme of circularity within his play. His ability to see his work in visual patterns led critics to label his directorial efforts as "choreography."

Although Beckett was a purist when it came to the language of his play, he somehow managed to balance his words with theatrical gestures. He instructed his actors to "Never let your changes of position and voice come together. First comes (a) the altered bodily stance; after it, following a slight pause, comes (b) the corresponding utterance." This was later referred to by critics as the step-by-step approach. Along with the other self-conscious devices incorporated into the dialogue, such as the elimination of the fourth wall, this gave *Waiting for Godot* its absurdly theatrical quality.

Pozzo's reference to the stage as the "Board," is followed by the "Black poetry" in his speech about giving birth "astride a grave." This is one of the only references to females in this play. And any positive sense of life renewing itself is dismissed swiftly. "They gave birth astride of a grave, the light gleams an instant, then it's "night once more." This is a play about men. "We are men," Vladimir states emphatically at the end of B-3, although it is immediately followed by Estragon's comment, "Sweet mother earth!"

Whatever Beckett's reasons were for excluding women from his play, he was adamant about it. During his life, he tried to close down productions with female casts. Since his death, any productions that do not follow his outline of the play are preceded by disclaimers.

Study Questions

1. Where are the men at the beginning of this section?

2. What does Estragon want to do now?

3. What does Vladimir do to Pozzo?

4. What does Pozzo do?

5. What names does Estragon use to call Pozzo?

6. After Estragon and Vladimir get up, what do they decide to do?

7. Why is Pozzo asking about the time?

8. How does Pozzo suggest that Estragon go about rousing Lucky?

9. What does Estragon do?

10. Why can't Lucky entertain the men as before?

Answers

1. The men are all on the ground.

2. Estragon wants to take a nap.

3. Vladimir hits Pozzo.

4. Pozzo cries out in pain and crawls away. He continues to call for help.

5. Estragon calls Pozzo "Abel", and then "Cain".

6. They decide to help Pozzo get up. When he falls, they help him up again, and support his body.

7. Pozzo is blind and has no conception of time.

8. Pozzo suggests that Estragon first pull on the rope. If that doesn't work, he should kick him in his face and in his groin.

9. Estragon starts yelling at Lucky, and kicking him. However, he hurts his own foot in the process.

10. Lucky cannot sing, think, or recite because he cannot speak anymore.

Suggested Essay Topics

1. Show how the biblical reference to Cain and Abel might apply to any or all of these characters.

2. Compare and contrast the ways in which all of these characters have been affected by the passage of time.

Act II, Section B-5

Summary

Vladimir and Estragon are alone. Vladimir awakens Estragon, does not want to hear his dream, and wonders about Pozzo's blindness. Estragon again asks if Pozzo was Godot.

Estragon's feet hurt. Vladimir ponders the "truth" of what happened, and what will continue to happen.

The boy enters. He doesn't recognize Vladimir and doesn't remember being there before. Vladimir knows the message by heart. He says it for the boy. He asks the boy about his brother. "He's sick, Sir," the boy says. Vladimir asks if Godot has a beard, if it's "fair" or "black." The boy replies, "I think it's white, Sir."

Again, the boy wants to know what to tell Godot. "Tell him you saw me...." Vladimir answers. Then he grabs the boy and warns him not to forget this meeting.

"The sun sets, the moon rises." Estragon gets up, removes his boots, puts them on the ground, and talks about leaving. Vladimir reminds him about Godot.

They look at the tree, and wonder if it's a willow. They would like to hang themselves. Estragon removes the cord from his waist that was holding up his pants. His pants fall down to his ankles.

They remain there while they test the strength of the cord. It breaks. Estragon says they can bring a stronger rope when they return. They agree to hang themselves unless Godot appears.

Vladimir tells Estragon to pull up his trousers. He does so. They decide to go, but they do not move.

Analysis

Although Section B-5 ends the play, it repeats elements of themes that have appeared throughout: waiting, nothingness, time, Godot, infirmities, pairing, pauses, silences, the two thieves, the step-by-step approach, and circularity. There is a subtle difference in the mood; there is a quality of hopelessness at the end. That becomes clear only through an informed reading of the play and the knowledge that nothing much has changed from beginning to end, not even the dialogue.

A-2
Estragon: Will you never let me sleep?
Vladimir: I felt lonely.
Estragon: I had a dream.
Vladimir: Don't tell me!

Estragon: I dreamt that—
Vladimir: DON'T TELL ME!

B-5
Estragon: Why will you never let me sleep?
Vladimir: I felt lonely.
Estragon: I was dreaming I was happy.
Vladimir: That passed the time.
Estragon: I was dreaming that—
Vladimir: (violently) Don't tell me!

Estragon remains barefoot at the end of the play. According to Beckett, his difficulty might be given a theological explanation. One of Estragon's feet is blessed, and the other damned. The boot will not go on the foot that is damned, but it will go on the foot that is blessed. That is why Estragon cries out in pain when he tries to walk. "I suppose I might as well get up. (He gets up painfully.) Ow! Didi!"

This idea of dualism, that the world is ruled by the antagonistic forces of good and evil, has been seen before. It can apply to the story of the "two thieves" from A-1, the reference Estragon makes to Cain and Abel in B-4, and the two brothers, one of whom is Godot's messenger.

By the end of the play, it is clear that Godot's arrival may not be a source of salvation for Estragon and Vladimir. They seemed to have sensed this before. The fear of his possible arrival causes Estragon to exclaim, "I'm accursed!" and "I'm in hell!" in B-2.

Again, subtle differences in the dialogue in A-2 and B-5 allude to this:

A-2
Estragon: Let's go.
Vladimir: We can't.
Estragon: Why not?
Vladimir: We're waiting for Godot.
Estragon: Ah! You're sure it was here?
Vladimir: What?
Estragon: That we were to wait.
Vladimir: He said by the tree. Do you see any others?

Estragon: What is it?
Vladimir: I don't know. A willow.
Estragon: Where are the leaves?
Vladimir: It must be dead.

B-5
Estragon: …let's go far away from here.
Vladimir: We can't
Estragon: Why not?
Vladimir: We have to come back tomorrow.
Estragon: What for?
Vladimir: To wait for Godot.
Estragon: Ah! He didn't come?

Vladimir: No.
Estragon: And now it's too late.
Vladimir: Yes, now it's night.
Estragon: And if we dropped him? If we dropped him?
Vladimir: He'd punish us. Everything's dead but the tree.
Estragon: What is it?
Vladimir: It's the tree.
Estragon: Yes, but what kind?
Vladimir: I don't know. A willow.

This exchange is also significant in the way it indicates the passage of time. The tree that seemed dead is now alive. The men are somewhat more aware than before, possibly by witnessing the dynamic between Pozzo and Lucky, that Godot, who seemed to offer a way out, might not prove to be such a benevolent master.

The essentials of A-6 and B-5 are the same. The men, as before, keep waiting for Godot. The boy brings the same message. In each section, suicide is planned for the next day. At the end of Act I, Estragon plans to bring a rope; at the end of Act II, he plans to bring a stronger rope.

Vladimir and Estragon grow more alike by the end of the play; the differences seemed blurred. They are both weary and discouraged. At the end of the first act, when Estragon brings up the idea of suicide, Vladimir lightens it up by suggesting, "It'd give us an erection." At the end of the second act, Vladimir concludes, "We'll hang ourselves tomorrow. Unless Godot comes."

In spite of the attempt at physical humor created when Estragon's pants fall down to his ankles, the second act ends on a more hopeless note than the first. The dialogue is exactly the same, except the speakers are reversed:

Estragon: Well, shall we go?
Vladimir: Yes, let's go.
They do not move.

Vladimir: Well? Shall we go?
Estragon: Yes, let's go.
They do not move.

It has been said about *Godot,* that because Act I and Act II follow the same pattern, "nothing happens—twice." However, a close and careful reading will prove that nothing happens, time and again.

Study Questions

1. What happens to Pozzo and Lucky after they leave?

2. What was Estragon's feeling in his dream?

3. What event has Estragon forgotten?

4. What does Vladimir know about Estragon's character?

5. Who arrives?

6. What is the difference between the way the boy delivers the message this time and the way it was done in A-6?

7. What happened to the boy's brother?

8. What new facts about Godot does the boy reveal?

9. What does Vladimir say will happen if the men forget about Godot?

10. What will they do when they return tomorrow?

Answers

1. After they leave, they fall down.

2. In his dream, he was feeling happy.

3. Estragon has forgotten that Lucky and Pozzo passed by again.

4. He knows that Estragon will awaken and remember nothing about what has happened. Estragon will complain about his injuries, and be hungry.

5. Godot's messenger arrives.

6. This time, Vladimir knows the message by heart, and says it himself. The boy merely confirms the facts.

7. The boy's brother is sick.

8. He describes Godot as having a white beard.

9. If the men choose to forget Godot, he may punish them.

10. They will try to hang themselves with a stronger rope, unless Godot arrives to save them.

Suggested Essay Topics

1. Estragon wants to tell Vladimir about his dream, but Vladimir does not want to hear about it. What does this indicate about each character?

2. What evidence is there that Godot might bring salvation? What evidence is there that he might not?

Sample Analytical Paper Topics

The following topics can be used for analytical papers on Samuel Beckett's *Waiting for Godot*. The outlines provide starting points for your writing.

Topic #1

This is a play about "Waiting." How is that evident throughout the play?

Outline

I.   Thesis Statement: *In this play, two characters wait for someone they call "Godot." While they wait on stage, the audience waits in their seats.*

II. Estragon and Vladimir wait by entertaining themselves with language.

    A.   The language of repetition

    B.   The language of double negatives

    C.   Vaudevillian "cross-talk"

    D.   Stichomythic play

    E.   Vladimir's songs

        1.   A "round song" in B-1

        2.   A lullaby in B-2

III. Estragon and Vladimir wait by playing games.

    A. In A-1 Vladimir says, "Come on, Gogo, return the ball"

        1. Back and forth rallying as on tennis court

        2. Words as balls

        3. In B-4, Estragon says "Child's play"

    B. In B-2, Vladimir and Estragon play "Pass the hat"

    C. In B-2, they play "Theater game." Vladimir says, "We could play at Pozzo and Lucky"

IV. Estragon and Vladimir wait, as spectators of the "play within a play"

    A. Evidence of breaking of "fourth wall"

    B. Vladimir's offstage antics

    C. Arrival of Pozzo and Lucky

V. The audience waits with physical themes of "Silence," and "Pause"

    A. Beckett said "If they did it my way, they would empty and theater"

    B. "Silence" follows dialogue

    C. "Pause" follows interactions of the characters

VI. Conclusion: "Waiting" is the essence of this play

Topic #2

Beckett called his play a "tragicomedy." What elements are there of tragedy? What elements are there of comedy? How are these elements interwoven?

Outline

I. Thesis Statement: *There are tragic elements as well as comic elements in this play. Tragic elements are seen in the circumstances of the characters, their life where "Nothing happens and*

*nothing can be done," and the empty stage. The comic elements
revolve around the games the characters invent, their interac-
tions with each other, and the vaudevillian routines.*

II. Tragic Elements

    A. Circumstances of the characters

        1. Vladimir and Estragon are homeless tramps

        2. Lucky as slave to Pozzo

            a. Lucky has a past that suggests he once could
               think, dance, recite and sing

            b. Lucky as a victim—akin to tortured prisoner

            c. Lucky loses his ability to speak

        3. Pozzo goes blind

    B. "Nothing happens and nothing can be done"

        1. The lives of Vladimir and Estragon never change

            a. They contemplate suicide

            b. They continue to wait for Godot

            c. They remain physically impaired

               1. Vladimir's bladder

               2. Estragon's feet

             d. They do not age

        2. Compared to Lucky

        3. Compared to Pozzo

    C. The empty stage

        1. The tree

        2. The mound

        3. The sky

        4. The moon

III. Comic Elements

    A. Language games

    B. Vaudevillian routines

    C. "All fall down" at the end of B-3

    D. Estragon's pants at the end of B-5

IV. Interwoven elements of tragedy and comedy

    A. Hopelessness becomes hopefulness

        1. Vladimir and Estragon continue to hope that salvation will come

        2. Pozzo and Lucky move on in spite of disabilities

    B. Humorous colloquialisms express tragic states

    C. Death does not arrive. The day passes

        1. The dead willow of Act I sprouts leaves by Act II

        2. The moon swiftly arrives at the end of both acts

V. Conclusion: This is a "tragicomedy" because elements of tragedy and comedy are clearly evident throughout the play

Topic #3

The characters in this play all function as part of what Beckett referred to as a "pseudocouple." Discuss the validity of this statement.

Outline

I. Thesis Statement: *Estragon and Vladimir function together as a couple. Pozzo and Lucky remain together as a couple. The boy, or messenger, has a brother so he is also part of a couple. Godot, who never arrives, is not a character in this play. He remains a "concept", and so he is not coupled.*

II. Estragon and Vladimir:

    A. Dependence on each other

    B. Validation of each other

    C. Sparring partners

    D. Knowledge of each other

    E.   Routines

    F.   Complementary infirmities

        1.   Vladimir's bladder; Estragon's feet

        2.   Vladimir's bad breath; Estragon's smelly feet

    G.   Complementary visual symbols

        1.   Vladimir's hat, tree and sky

        2.   Estragon's boots, mound, and ground

III. Pozzo and Lucky

    A.   Master-Slave relationship

    B.   Sado-masochistic relationship

    C.   Complementary patterns of aging

        1.   Pozzo's blindness

        2.   Lucky's inability to speak

IV. The boy and his brother

    A.   Employed by Godot

        1.   As messengers

        2.   As goatherd and shepherd

    B.   Good and evil

        1.   One is beaten

        2.   One is not

V. Godot remains unknown

    A.   Estragon and Vladimir project that he has consultants in A-2

    B.   The boy describes his physical attributes and behavioral patterns

    C.   He never appears, so he remains a concept

    D.   The concept is open-ended, and lends itself to numerous interpretations

1. Godot as God
2. Godot as Pozzo
3. Godot according to critics and scholars

VI. Conclusion: There is great validity to the idea of the "pseudo-couple" in this play.

Topic #4

William Blake, an English poet who lived from 1757 to 1827, believed that man's psyche consisted of four elements—imagination, reason, passion, and bodily sensation. While the ideal man could maintain a balance of these four elements, evil resulted from the fact that most men couldn't. The characters in *Waiting for Godot* have been said to represent these four elements of the psyche. Discuss this idea.

Outline

I.   Thesis Statement: *The four elements of man's psyche are represented by Pozzo (sensations), Lucky (thought), Vladimir (feeling), and Estragon (imagination). At times they are at peace with one another, and at time they are at war.*

II. Pozzo Represents Sensations

    A. Enslavement of Lucky

        1. Cracking of whip.

        2. Jerking of rope.

    B. Material possesions

        1. Heavy bag

        2. Folding stool

        3. Picnic basket

        4. Overcoat

        5. Whip

        6. Rope around Lucky's neck

      7. Glasses

      8. Pocket watch

      9. Pipe and tobacco

     10. Matches

     11. Vaporizer

     12. Handkerchief

     13. Hat

C. Mannerisms and Affectations

      1. Loud voice

      2. Enormous laugh

      3. Magnanimous gestures

      4. Pomp and circumstance

D. Consumption of food

      1. Drinking from wine bottle

      2. Sucking on chicken bones

III. Lucky Represents Thought

A. Past Life

      1. As Pozzo's teacher

      2. As a dancer

      3. As a singer

      4. As an orator

B. Present Existence

      1. Pozzo's slave

      2. General deterioration of his body—weak and decrepit

      3. Discontinuous movements—The Net

      4. Lucky's speech

          a. Repeated phrases

          b. Broken sentences

      c.   Manic confusion

      d.   Disjointed images

IV. Vladimir Represents Feeling

    A.   Closeness to Estragon

    B.   Religious Sentiments

      1.   Repentance

      2.   Four Evangelists

      3.   Salvation

    C.   Reaction to Pozzo's Treatment of Lucky

    D.   Misery of Isolation

V. Estragon Represents Imagination

    A.   Past Life as a Poet

    B.   Sleeping and Dreaming

    C.   Suicidal Impulses

    D.   No Sense of Time

    E.   Memory Loss

    F.   Tragic and Endless Existence

    G.   Meaningless Life

VI. Pozzo and Lucky Function as a Couple

VII. Pozzo and Lucky Share Sado-Masochistic Relationship

VIII. Vladimir and Estragon are Dependent on Each Other

IX. Vladimir and Estragon Quarrel Incessantly

X. Pozzo Attempts to Take Control

XI. All Fall Down

    A.   Equality After Lucky's Speech

    B.   Silence and Pause

XII. Conclusion: Pozzo, Lucky, Vladimir, and Estragon can be compared to the four elements of the psyche. At times they are at peace with each other; and at times they are at war with each other.

Topic #5

In 1988, Frank Rich, a theatrical reviewer for *The New York TImes,* wrote, "...no play could be more elemental in either form or content. 'Godot' speaks equally to prison inmates and university students because it reduces the task of existence to its humblest essentials: eating, excretion, sleeping, companionship, waiting anxiously for life to reach some point (whatever that point may be)." Discuss the validity of this statement as it relates to the setting of the play as well as to the main characters, Vladimir and Estragon.

Outline

I.   Thesis Statement: *In form and content,* Waiting for Godot, *demonstrates the simple existence of its main characters, Vladimir and Estragon. They exist on a bare stage with a mound and a tree while they wait for someone named Godot.*

II. Simplicity of the setting

    A.   The play takes place on a country road.

        1.   There is a mound.

        2.   There is a tree.

            a.   Without leaves in Act I

            b.   With a few leaves in Act II

    B.   It is evening

        1.   Moon rises at the end of Act I

        2.   Sun sets and moon rises at the end of Act II

III. Simplicity of life for Vladimir and Estragon

    A.   Eating

        1.   Vladimir provides food from his pockets

            a.   Turnips

        b.   Carrots

        c.   Black radish

    2. Estragon eats

        a.   Vladimir's food

        b.   Pozzo's chicken bones

B. Excretion

    1. Vladimir has difficulty with his bladder

    2. Vladimir relieves himself offstage

    3. Estragon and Vladimir's conversation

C. Sleeping

    1. Estragon sleeps in a ditch

    2. Estragon gets beaten by strangers

    3. Estragon naps onstage

D. Companionship

    1. Vladimir and Estragon complement each other.

    2. They argue but remain together.

E. Waiting

    1. They wait for Godot.

    2. They wait for a change in their lives.

IV. Simplicity of Actions

  A. Pozzo and Lucky come and go in Act I

  B. Pozzo and Lucky come and go in Act II

  C. Nothing changes for Vladimir and Estragon

V. Conclusion: Life for Vladimir and Estragon is broken down into its simplest form. It consists of eating, excretion, sleeping, companionship, and waiting. Nothing happens to them or to their surroundings.

Topic #6

It has been said that language is the essence of this play. Using Ruby Cohn's terminology, discuss this statement.

Outline

I.   Thesis Statement: *Ruby Cohn discusses the language of* Waiting for Godot *in her book,* Just Play: Beckett's Theater. *She creates categories for much of the dialogue of the characters.*

II. The dialogue is repetitious.

    A. Simple Doublets

    B. Interrupted Doublets

    C. Distanced Doublets

    D. Echo Doublets

    E. Triplets

    F. Multiplets

    G. Pounders

    H. Volleys

    I. Refrains

    J. Repeated Negatives

III. Conclusion: The language in *Waiting for Godot* is repetitious. It can be analyzed according to the categories defined by Ruby Cohn, Beckett scholar and author.

SECTION FIVE

Bibliography

Alvarez, A. (1973). Samuel Beckett. New York: Viking Press.

Atkinson, B. (1956, April 20). Theatre: Beckett's *Waiting for Godot.* *The New York Times,* p. 21.

Bair, D. (1978). *Samuel Beckett: A Biography.* United States: Harcourt Brace Jovanovich.

Beckett, Samuel. (1954). *The Collected Works of Samuel Beckett: Waiting for Godot.* (3rd printing, 1978). New York: Grove Press.

Beckett, Samuel. (1953). *Watt.* New York: Grove Press.

Ben-Zvi, L. (1986). *Samuel Beckett.* Boston: Twayne Publishers.

Bloom, H. (Ed.). (1987). *Modern Critical interpretations: Samuel Beckett's Waiting for Godot.* New York: Chelsea House.

Braun, S. (1989, December 27). Samuel Beckett Dies at 83; "Godot" Author, Nobelist. *The Los Angeles Times,* p.1.

Cohn, R. (1973). *Back to Beckett.* Princeton: Princeton University Press.

Cohn, R. (1980). *Just Play: Beckett's Theater.* Princeton: Princeton University Press.

Donoghue, D. (1986). *We Irish.* New York: Alfred A. Knopf.

Esslin, M. (1961). *The Theatre of the Absurd.* New York: Doubleday.

Fletcher, J., & Spurling, J. (1985). *Beckett the Playwright.* New York: Hill & Wang.

Gontarski, S. E. (Ed.). (1986). *On Beckett: Essays and Criticisms.* New York: Grove Press.

Gontarski, S. E. (Ed.). (1992) *The Theatrical Notebooks of Samuel Beckett: Endgame.* New York: Grove Press.

Guicharnaud, J. (1967). *Modern French Theatre.* New Haven: Yale University Press.

Kalb, J. (1989). *Beckett in Performance.* Cambridge: Cambridge University Press.

Kennedy, A. (1989). *Samuel Beckett.* Cambridge: Cambridge University Press.

McMillan, D. & Fehsenfeld, M. (1988). *Beckett in the Theatre.* London: John Calder.

Mobley, J. P. (1992). *NTC's Dictionary of Theatre and Drama Terms.* Illinois: National Textbook Company.

Montague, J. (1994, April 17). A Few Drinks and a Hymn: My Farewell to Samuel Beckett. *The New York Times Book Review,* p. 24.

O'Brian, E. (1986). *The Beckett Country.* Dublin: The Black Cat Press Limited.

Topics of the Times: The Rites of Godot (1988, November 21). *The New York Times,* page 18.

Available at your local bookstore or order directly from us by sending in coupon below.

MAXnotes®

REA's Literature Study Guides

MAXnotes® are student-friendly. They offer a fresh look at masterpieces of literature, presented in a lively and interesting fashion. **MAXnotes®** offer the essentials of what you should know about the work, including outlines, explanations and discussions of the plot, character lists, analyses, and historical context. **MAXnotes®** are designed to help you think independently about literary works by raising various issues and thought-provoking ideas and questions. Written by literary experts who currently teach the subject, **MAXnotes®** enhance your understanding and enjoyment of the work.

Available **MAXnotes®** include the following:

Absalom, Absalom!
The Aeneid of Virgil
Animal Farm
Antony and Cleopatra
As I Lay Dying
As You Like It
The Autobiography of
	Malcolm X
The Awakening
Beloved
Beowulf
Billy Budd
The Bluest Eye, A Novel
Brave New World
The Canterbury Tales
The Catcher in the Rye
The Color Purple
The Crucible
Death in Venice
Death of a Salesman
The Divine Comedy I: Inferno
Dubliners
Emma
Euripedes' Electra & Medea
Frankenstein
Gone with the Wind
The Grapes of Wrath
Great Expectations
The Great Gatsby
Gulliver's Travels
Hamlet
Hard Times

Heart of Darkness
Henry IV, Part I
Henry V
The House on Mango Street
Huckleberry Finn
I Know Why the Caged
	Bird Sings
The Iliad
Invisible Man
Jane Eyre
Jazz
The Joy Luck Club
Jude the Obscure
Julius Caesar
King Lear
Les Misérables
Lord of the Flies
Macbeth
The Merchant of Venice
The Metamorphoses of Ovid
The Metamorphosis
Middlemarch
A Midsummer Night's Dream
Moby-Dick
Moll Flanders
Mrs. Dalloway
Much Ado About Nothing
My Antonia
Native Son
1984
The Odyssey
Oedipus Trilogy

Of Mice and Men
On the Road
Othello
Paradise Lost
A Passage to India
Plato's Republic
Portrait of a Lady
A Portrait of the Artist
	as a Young Man
Pride and Prejudice
A Raisin in the Sun
Richard II
Romeo and Juliet
The Scarlet Letter
Sir Gawain and the
	Green Knight
Slaughterhouse-Five
Song of Solomon
The Sound and the Fury
The Stranger
The Sun Also Rises
A Tale of Two Cities
Taming of the Shrew
The Tempest
Tess of the D'Urbervilles
Their Eyes Were Watching God
To Kill a Mockingbird
To the Lighthouse
Twelfth Night
Uncle Tom's Cabin
Waiting for Godot
Wuthering Heights

RESEARCH & EDUCATION ASSOCIATION
61 Ethel Road W. • Piscataway, New Jersey 08854
Phone: (908) 819-8880

Please send me more information about MAXnotes®.

Name _____

Address _____

City _____ State _____ Zip _____